CONTENTS

0. Foreword

1. The basics of starting a business: From idea generation to legal requirements, this chapter could cover everything a potential entrepreneur needs to know before starting a business.

2. Financing options for small businesses: This chapter could cover traditional financing options like bank loans and grants, as well as newer options like crowd funding and peer-to-peer lending.

3. Financial management: This chapter could cover the basics of managing business finances, including budgeting, accounting, and taxation.

4. Marketing and sales: This chapter could cover the importance of marketing and sales in growing a business, as well as various strategies for attracting and retaining customers.

5. Scaling a business: This chapter could cover the strategies for growing a business to achieve greater success, including hiring employees, outsourcing, and expanding into new   markets.

6. Investing and wealth management: This chapter could cover the basics of investing and wealth management, including how to create a diversified portfolio and the importance   of   long-term   investing.

7. Entrepreneurial mindset: This chapter could cover the mindset and qualities necessary for success as an entrepreneur,   including   resilience,   creativity,   and   a willingness   to   take   calculated   risks.

8. Case studies and success stories: Including case studies and success stories of successful entrepreneurs and businesses can help inspire readers and provide practical examples of how to apply the concepts covered in the book.

9. Future trends in business and finance: Including a chapter on future trends in business and finance can help readers stay up-to-date on the latest developments and prepare   for   future   changes   in   the   industry.

10. Additional resources: Including a list of additional resources, such as books, websites, and podcasts, can help readers continue learning and growing even after finishing the book.

Foreword

In today's fast-paced and ever-changing business landscape, it can be challenging to navigate the complex world of finance and entrepreneurship. With so many different strategies and approaches to choose from, it can be difficult to know where to begin when it comes to achieving success and profitability.

That's where "Profitable Pathways: Strategies for Business and Financial Success" comes in. This book offers a comprehensive guide to the most effective and proven strategies for building and growing a successful business, increasing profits, and achieving financial stability.

Drawing on decades of experience in the business world, our expert authors have compiled a wealth of practical advice and actionable insights to help you navigate the challenges of entrepreneurship and finance. Whether you're a seasoned business owner looking to take your company to the next level, or a new entrepreneur just starting out, this book has something to offer.

From mastering the art of financial management and budgeting, to developing effective marketing and sales strategies, to building a strong team and culture, "Profitable Pathways" covers all the key elements of business success. With real-world case studies and practical tips and advice, this book is an essential resource for anyone looking to achieve profitability and financial stability in today's competitive business environment.

So if you're ready to take your business to the next level and achieve lasting success, "Profitable Pathways" is the guide you need to get there.

Chapter 1

The basics of starting a business:

1. Idea generation: This section could cover how to come up with a viable business idea and evaluate its potential for success. It could also discuss how to test and validate a business idea before committing to it.

2. Market research: This section could cover the importance of market research in understanding customer needs and preferences, as well as identifying potential competitors and market trends.

3. Business planning: This section could cover how to create a business plan, including the key components of a business plan such as executive summary, marketing plan, financial projections, and operational plan.

4. Legal requirements: This section could cover the various legal requirements for starting a business, including registering the business, obtaining necessary permits and licenses, and complying with tax laws and regulations.

5. Funding options: This section could cover the various financing options available to entrepreneurs, including traditional loans, government grants, venture capital, and crowdfunding.

6. Business structure: This section could cover the different types of business structures available, including sole proprietorships, partnerships, limited liability companies (LLCs), and corporations, and the advantages and disadvantages of each structure.

7. Branding and marketing: This section could cover the importance of branding and marketing in building a successful business, including how to develop a brand identity and create a marketing plan.

8. Sales and customer service: This section could cover the basics of sales and customer service, including how to attract and retain customers, build relationships, and provide excellent customer service.

9. Operations and logistics: This section could cover the basics of operations and logistics, including how to manage inventory, fulfill orders, and streamline business processes.

10. Human resources: This section could cover how to hire and manage employees, including how to create job descriptions, conduct interviews, and provide training and development opportunities.

Chapter 2

Financing options for small businesses:

1. Traditional financing options: This section could cover the various traditional financing options available to small businesses, such as bank loans, lines of credit, and Small Business Administration (SBA) loans. It could discuss the advantages and disadvantages of each option and provide guidance on how to choose the best option for a particular business.

2. Grants: This section could cover how to find and apply for grants for small businesses, including government grants, private foundation grants, and corporate grants.

3. Crowd funding: This section could cover the basics of crowd funding, including how it works, the different types of crowd funding, and how to launch a successful crowd funding campaign.

4. Peer-to-peer lending: This section could cover the basics of peer-to-peer lending, including how it differs from traditional financing options and the advantages and disadvantages of using peer-to-peer lending platforms.

5. Equity financing: This section could cover the basics of equity financing, including how it works, the different types of equity financing, and how to prepare for an equity financing round.

6. Alternative financing options: This section could cover newer and alternative financing options available to small businesses, such as revenue-based financing, factoring, and merchant cash advances.

7. Financial statements and creditworthiness: This section could cover the importance of financial statements and creditworthiness in securing financing for a small business. It could provide guidance on how to prepare financial statements and improve creditworthiness.

8. Due diligence and legal considerations: This section could cover the due diligence and legal considerations involved in securing financing, including how to prepare a business plan and pitch deck, and how to negotiate financing terms with investors or lenders.

Readers will have a comprehensive understanding of the various financing options available to small businesses and how to choose the best option for their particular needs.

Chapter 3

Financial management

Financial management is a critical aspect of running a successful business. It involves managing the financial resources of the company, including budgeting, accounting, and taxation. In this chapter, we will explore the basics of financial management and provide guidance on how to effectively manage business finances.

Section 1: Budgeting

Budgeting is the process of creating a financial plan for the business. It involves estimating the revenue and expenses for a specific period, such as a month or a year. The budget should be realistic and based on the business's historical performance, industry trends, and growth projections. This section will cover the key components of a budget, including revenue sources, fixed and variable expenses, and cash flow projections.

Section 2: Accounting

Accounting is the process of recording, classifying, and summarizing financial transactions. It provides a clear and accurate picture of the company's financial performance and helps in making informed business decisions. This section will cover the basics of accounting, including the accounting equation, financial statements, and the use of accounting software.

Section 3: Taxation

Taxation is a complex area that can have a significant impact on the financial health of the business. It is essential to understand the tax laws and regulations that apply to the business, including income tax, sales tax, and payroll tax. This section will cover the basics of taxation, including tax planning, tax compliance, and tax reporting.

Section 4: Financial Analysis

Financial analysis is the process of evaluating the financial performance of the business. It involves analyzing financial statements, such as the balance sheet and income statement, to identify trends and areas for improvement. This section will cover the key financial ratios and metrics used in financial analysis, such as profitability ratios, liquidity ratios, and efficiency ratios.

Section 5: Financing

Financing is the process of obtaining funding for the business. It can be challenging to secure financing, especially for new businesses. This section will cover the various sources of financing available to the business, including equity financing, debt financing, and alternative financing options.

In conclusion, financial management is a critical aspect of running a successful business. By following the guidelines provided in this chapter, entrepreneurs can effectively manage their finances and make informed business decisions that will help them achieve their goals and succeed in their chosen industry.

Chapter 4

Marketing and sales:

Marketing and sales are critical components of growing a successful business. Effective marketing and sales strategies can help businesses attract and retain customers, build brand awareness, and increase revenue. In this chapter, we will explore the importance of marketing and sales and provide guidance on various strategies for attracting and retaining customers.

Section 1:   Understanding Your Target Market

Understanding your target market is the first step in developing an effective marketing and sales strategy. This section will cover the importance of identifying your target market, including their needs, preferences, and behaviors. It will also cover the various methods for conducting market research, such as surveys, focus groups, and customer feedback.

Section 2:   Developing a Marketing Strategy

A marketing strategy is a comprehensive plan for promoting your products or services to your target market. This section will cover the key components of a marketing strategy, including branding, advertising, public relations, and social media. It will also cover the various marketing channels available to businesses, including online and offline marketing.

Section 3:   Sales   Strategies

Sales strategies are the tactics used to convert potential customers into paying customers. This section will cover the various sales strategies available to businesses, including direct sales, channel sales, and online sales. It will also cover the importance of customer relationship management and the use of sales analytics to track and improve sales performance.

Section 4:   Customer Retention Strategies

Customer retention is the process of keeping existing customers engaged and satisfied with your products or services. This section will cover the various customer retention strategies available to businesses, including loyalty programs, customer feedback, and personalized marketing. It will also cover the importance of customer service and the role it plays in   customer   retention.

Section 5: Measuring Marketing and Sales Performance

Measuring marketing and sales performance is essential for identifying areas for improvement and evaluating the effectiveness of your marketing and sales strategies. This section will cover the various metrics used to measure marketing and sales performance, including customer acquisition cost, conversion rate, and customer lifetime value. It will also cover the use of marketing and sales analytics to track and analyze marketing and sales data.

In conclusion, marketing and sales are critical components of growing a successful business. By following the guidelines provided in this chapter, entrepreneurs can develop effective marketing and sales strategies that will help them attract and retain customers, build brand awareness, and increase revenue.

Chapter5.

Scaling a business:

Scaling a business refers to the process of growing a business in order to achieve greater success. This chapter will cover various strategies for scaling a business, including hiring employees, outsourcing, and expanding into new markets.

Section 1: Hiring Employees

One of the primary strategies for scaling a business is hiring employees. This can help a business increase its productivity, expand its capabilities, and take on more work. However, hiring employees also comes with several challenges, such as finding the right talent, managing and training employees, and providing benefits and compensation.

This section will cover topics such as:

- When to hire employees and how to determine the right number and type of employees for your business

- Strategies for attracting and retaining top talent

- Best practices for onboarding and training new employees

- Managing employee performance and providing feedback

- Developing competitive compensation and benefits packages

Section 2:   Outsourcing

Outsourcing is another strategy for scaling a business, which involves contracting out certain business functions to external vendors or service providers. Outsourcing can be a cost-effective way to access specialized skills, expertise, and resources, while also allowing the business to focus on its core competencies.

This   section   will   cover   topics   such   as:

- Identifying which business functions are suitable for outsourcing

- Finding and selecting the right outsourcing partners

- Establishing effective communication and collaboration with outsourcing   partners

- Managing outsourcing contracts and ensuring quality control

Section 3:   Expanding   into   New   Markets

Expanding into new markets is a strategy for scaling a business that can help increase revenue and reach new customers. This can involve expanding geographically, entering new product or service categories, or targeting new customer segments.

This   section   will   cover   topics   such   as:

- Conducting market research to identify new opportunities
-     Developing   a   market   entry   strategy
- Adapting products and services to meet the needs of new markets
- Building brand awareness and establishing a presence in new markets
- Managing the risks and challenges of expanding into new markets, such as regulatory compliance, cultural differences, and competition.

Conclusion:

Scaling a business is a complex process that requires careful planning, execution, and ongoing evaluation. By leveraging strategies such as hiring employees, outsourcing, and expanding into new markets, businesses can achieve greater success and fulfill their growth potential.

Chapter 6.

Investing and wealth management:

Investing and wealth management are critical components of financial planning, and this chapter will cover the basics of both. It will provide an overview of investing, including the types of investments available, how to create a diversified portfolio, and the importance of long-term investing. It will also cover the fundamentals of wealth management, including how to manage your finances, reduce debt, and build wealth over time.

Section 1:   Investing

Investing is the process of allocating money to various assets with the expectation of generating a return. This section will cover the basics of investing, including:

- Understanding the different types of investments, such as stocks, bonds, mutual funds, and exchange-traded funds (ETFs)
- Determining your investment goals and risk tolerance
- Creating a diversified portfolio to manage risk and maximize returns
- Evaluating investment performance and making adjustments as needed
- Understanding the role of taxes and fees in investing

Section 2:   Wealth Management

Wealth management is the process of managing your financial resources to achieve your financial goals. This section will cover the basics of wealth management, including:

- Creating a budget and managing your cash flow

- Reducing debt and improving your credit score

- Creating an emergency fund to manage unexpected expenses

- Saving for retirement and other long-term goals

- Managing risk through insurance and other risk management strategies

-    Building   and   preserving   wealth   over   time

Section 3:   Long-Term   Investing

Long-term investing is a key component of wealth management and involves investing for a period of five years or longer. This section will cover the importance of long-term investing, including:

- Understanding the benefits of long-term investing, such as the power of compounding and the ability to weather market fluctuations

- Developing a long-term investment strategy that aligns with your goals and risk tolerance

- Avoiding common mistakes that can derail long-term investment success, such as reacting to short-term market fluctuations or trying to time the market

Conclusion:

Investing and wealth management are critical components of financial planning, and this chapter has covered the basics of both. By understanding the different types of investments, creating a diversified portfolio, and focusing on long-term investing, individuals can build wealth over time and achieve their financial goals. By managing their finances effectively, reducing debt, and investing wisely, individuals can create a solid financial foundation for themselves and their families.

Chapter 7.

Entrepreneurial mindset:

Introduction:

Entrepreneurship is a challenging and rewarding journey that requires a unique set of skills and attributes. In this chapter, we will explore the mindset and qualities necessary for success as an entrepreneur.

Section 1: Understanding the Entrepreneurial Mindset

- Definition of an entrepreneurial mindset

- Characteristics of successful entrepreneurs

- Importance of developing an entrepreneurial mindset

Section 2: Key Qualities of Successful Entrepreneurs

- Resilience and Perseverance

- Creativity and Innovation

- Risk-Taking and Calculated Decision Making

- Adaptability and Flexibility

- Passion and Drive

Section 3: Ways to Develop an Entrepreneurial Mindset

- Seeking out mentorship and guidance

- Building a network of like-minded individuals

- Embracing failure and learning from mistakes

- Practicing self-reflection and mindfulness

- Continuously learning and seeking out new experiences

Section 4: Overcoming Obstacles and Challenges
- Dealing with uncertainty and ambiguity

- Managing stress and anxiety

- Maintaining motivation and focus

- Overcoming fear of failure

Conclusion:

Developing an entrepreneurial mindset is crucial for success as an entrepreneur. By understanding the key qualities and characteristics of successful entrepreneurs and actively working to develop these traits, anyone can cultivate an entrepreneurial mindset and increase their chances of success in the world of entrepreneurship.

Chapter 8.

Case studies and success stories:

Introduction:

Learning from the experiences of successful entrepreneurs can be an invaluable way to gain insights into the world of entrepreneurship. In this chapter, we will explore case studies and success stories of successful entrepreneurs and businesses.

Section 1: Case Studies of Successful Entrepreneurs

- Steve Jobs and   Apple

- Elon Musk and   Tesla

- Oprah Winfrey and OWN   Network

- Sara Blakely and   Spanx

- Jeff Bezos and   Amazon

Section 2: Success Stories of Small Businesses

- Warby Parker: Disrupting the Eyewear Industry

- Airbnb: Creating a New Market for Short-Term Rentals

- Patagonia: Combining Sustainability and Profitability

- TOMS: One-for-One Model for Social Impact

- Sweetgreen: Revolutionizing Fast Food

Section 3: Lessons Learned from Successful Entrepreneurs

- Identifying and solving a problem

- Building a strong team

- Embracing innovation and disruption

- Focusing on customer satisfaction

- Balancing short-term goals with long-term vision

Section 4: Applying Lessons Learned to Your Own Entrepreneurial Journey

- Identifying opportunities for innovation and disruption

- Building a strong network and team

- Prioritizing customer satisfaction and feedback

- Balancing short-term goals with long-term vision

- Embracing failure as a learning opportunity

Conclusion:

Case studies and success stories of successful entrepreneurs and businesses can provide valuable insights and inspiration for anyone looking to embark on their own entrepreneurial journey. By learning from the experiences of others, we can gain a better understanding of the mindset and strategies necessary for success in the world of entrepreneurship.

Chapter 9.

Future trends in business and finance:

Introduction:

The world of business and finance is constantly evolving, and staying up-to-date on the latest trends and developments is essential for success. In this chapter, we will explore some of the most significant future trends in business and finance and discuss how they will impact the industry.

Section 1: Technology and   Innovation

- The rise of artificial intelligence and machine learning

- Blockchain technology and cryptocurrency

- The Internet of Things (IoT) and connected devices

- Augmented and virtual reality

Section 2: Social and Environmental Responsibility

- Corporate social responsibility and sustainability

- Impact investing and social entrepreneurship

- The circular economy and zero-waste initiatives

Section 3: Changes in Consumer Behavior

- The rise of e-commerce and online marketplaces

- Personalization and customization of products and services

- The shift towards conscious consumption and ethical purchasing

Section 4: Regulation and Policy

- Changes in tax laws and regulations

- The impact of geopolitical events on the global economy

- Government policies and initiatives to promote

entrepreneurship and innovation

Section 5: The Future of Work

- The rise of remote work and the gig economy

- The impact of automation on jobs and the workforce

- The importance of upskilling and reskilling for career advancement

Conclusion:

Staying ahead of the curve in the world of business and finance requires a keen eye for emerging trends and the ability to adapt to changing circumstances. By understanding the future trends outlined in this chapter, readers can better prepare themselves and their businesses for the challenges and opportunities that lie ahead.

Chapter 10:

Additional Resources for Continued Learning and Growth

Introduction:

The journey towards business and financial success is ongoing, and there are always new insights and perspectives to be gained. In this chapter, we will provide a list of additional resources to help readers continue their learning and growth beyond the pages of this book.

Section 1:   Books

- The Lean Startup by Eric Ries

- Good to Great by Jim Collins

- The 7 Habits of Highly Effective People by Stephen Covey

- The Power of Habit by Charles Duhigg

- The Four Hour Work Week by Timothy Ferriss

Section 2: Websites and   Blogs

- Entrepreneur.com

- Forbes.com

- Inc.com

- FastCompany.com

- HBR.org

Section 3:   Podcasts

- How I Built This with Guy Raz

- The Tim Ferriss Show

- Masters of Scale with Reid Hoffman

- The GaryVee Audio Experience

- StartUp by Gimlet　　　Media

Section 4: Online Courses and Training

- Udemy.com

- Coursera.org

- LinkedIn　　　Learning

- Skillshare.com

- edX.org

Section 5: Professional Networks and Organizations

- Young Entrepreneur Council　　　(YEC)
- Entrepreneurs' Organization　　　(EO)
- National Association of Small Business Owners (NASBO)
- Small Business Administration　　(SBA)
- Chamber of　Commerce

Conclusion:

By tapping into the resources listed in this chapter, readers can continue to learn, grow and develop their skills and knowledge, even after finishing the book. Whether through books, websites, podcasts, online courses, or professional networks, there are countless opportunities to continue building towards business and financial success.

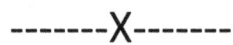

-------X-------